UNLIMITED NATURE

DARSH SATHCHITH

INDIA • SINGAPORE • MALAYSIA

ISBN 979-8-89475-391-1

CONTENTS

Contents

Contents

Unlimited Nature

In the world we live in, what do you see? Buildings, machines, power plants, sky scarpers, wind mills and solar panels. But have you ever wondered what animals, birds, trees, reptiles, plants could be there in the wild? Well wonder no more we're going on a trip across the world!

Our first destination is...............

THE AFRICAN SAVANNAH

The African Savannah is a huge grassland filled with various types of animals such as giraffes, lions, honey badgers, zebras, hippos, rhinos, elephants etc.

GIRAFFES

Giraffes are long necked mammals with large and powerful hearts- and by large heart I don't mean that giraffes are the most generous creatures in the world!!! I mean they literally have large hearts to pump the blood all the way up to their head from their chest. Giraffes have long necks due to two reasons- one, they are used to reach leaves high up in trees and two, to battle other male giraffes to show the female their dominance and to win the female's trust. They have long tongues to grab the leaves easily. This also means they can get past all the thorns on the tree branches. Now most people don't think too much about a giraffe's leg which is a shame as they are the reason the giraffe is alive! The reason for this is legs help the giraffe defend against predators as one swipe could injure a lion, that is if the lion does'nt go for a *crit which it rarely does. One animal that can kill a giraffe is the African leopard as it has the ability to jump down from a tree and attack a giraffe's vital organs. Another animal that can kill a giraffe is the hyena, as it can lock a deadly*crit that could shatter bones!

*Crit- Short for Critical hit

Lion

Lions are formidable threats in the savannah. With their strong and muscular bodies they can land heavy blows to anything that is not far above its weight class and this becomes more impressive when you compare it to other animals such as aardwolves and hyenas. But then in speed it has some tricky competitors like animals such as cheetahs and ostriches. When it comes to strength, the strong mammal loses by a huge margin like the hippopotamus, rhinoceros and elephant. In comparison to other predators, pythons are the only predators that are actually capable of injuring or at least giving the lion second thoughts. As for other predatory animals, the lion outmatches all of them except for the hyena. It might be competition for the lion as even though a lion is big and strong and is able to stand up for itself, a lion which is alone could easily be defeated by a pack of hyenas. But if a pride of lions meet a pack of hyenas, the lions will win with no doubt! Honey Badgers are also capable of defeating lions.

That was a bit about the lion's place in the food chain. Now we will talk about its life. Now, small lion cubs are born and raised in the pride. For female lion cubs, this is true. But for males, after a certain age, they will be thrown out of the group. This is because, when the lion grows up, it will fight with its father for the position of pride leader. But females would not do that. Only apes are smart enough to see virtually no difference between boys and girls. So after the lion is expelled, from the pride, all of its learnings will come in very handy as it tries and fails countless time to catch its own food. Now, here is something very funny. The expelled lions from the same pride or different pride can form a group called coalition and work together to get a pride that they can rule together.

Here's an example- The cub of a lion is sort of like Oliver Twist!! His mother stopped people from trying to kill him by orphaning him and then our lion cub or Oliver, will find some friends and get a new home.

Honey Badger

(Honey Badger attacking antelope)

Honey Badgers are small but they are fierce. They are the toughest animals in Africa. They are such good fighters that not even a lion can stand up to them. By that I don't mean that the lion will run away from the honey badgers, the lion will definitely put up a fight. The honey badger will keep on fighting with the lion till it decides to give up. People have still not figured out whether the honey badger is a herbivore or carnivore. Honey badgers eat honey but some say that the honey badgers are carnivores. They have thick fur protecting their neck from scratches, bites or injuries. The fur also helps it while battling with predators.

Fun fact- Honey badgers are members of the skunk family, as in, they are able to create a horrible smell that could ward away bees when they come looking for honey! Also, both skunks and honey badgers belong to the family of mustelids which include the wolverine and giant river otter. This group of animals was an offshoot of the dog and bear factions. The mustelids involve creatures like the weasel, wolverine, squirrels and rodents. This group has been particularly made to keep the bears and dogs in check.

Zebras

A lot of you know what a zebra is, now let us get to the part where I talk about some interesting things about them. The Zebras have their black and white colour to confuse predators with their stripes, so that the predators won't know one zebra from another. They always move around in herds, and get really spooked by any sudden noises and start stampeding. The young ones might not always keep up with the herd and sometimes may get left behind. But most of the time, the female zebras ensure that their young ones are following them. In rare cases the young ones might get separated from the herd. Once left alone, the young zebras are very vulnerable to predators such as lions, cheetahs and jaguars. Another interesting fact about zebras are their patriarchal displays which basically means 2 male zebras fighting against each other to be the leader of the herd. These fights sometimes result in death where neither opponent chooses to withdraw from the tense battle. But in most instances, these duels end with one zebra backing away. In most cases this is the slightly older and more experienced one. Now, you might be thinking the male zebras in the herd might fight each other, right? That is not true. As there is only one male in the group, and young male zebras in the herd are kicked out.

Fun fact: Zebras are actually black in colour with white stripes on their body and how you know this is by simply looking at a Zebra's nose. The hair on it is black. Meaning, the zebras have a black undercoat and there are white stripes on top.

HIPPOPOTAMUS

The hippopotamus is the 3rd largest land animal. At first glance the hippopotamus might appear harmless but it is actually very territorial and defends its homes fiercely. They have large teeth which they use to defend themselves from crocodiles and other hippopotamuses. They are so territorial that they don't even share their ponds with Zebras. Not even lions can defeat these fearsome mammals. With all these facts, you might think hippos are carnivores, but they are actually grass eaters. They stay in their pond at day time because their skin would get dry otherwise and then their skin would also get exposed to the harmful rays from the Sun. At night when it's cool and dark, the hippopotamuses come out of the water and then eat grass. In case they face any predators such as a lion pride, they would flee to the water for safety. Even though they are very territorial, some animals such as elephants can beat them in a fight. Elephants are the only animals that the hippopotamuses will not try to bother as they do not stand a chance against the mighty elephant. Rhinoceroses are equally matched with hippopotamuses. Other animals such as lions, cheetahs, gazelles, giraffes and antelopes will have a tough time getting past the hippos without attracting their attention. In case a pride of lions attacks a lone hippo, the lion pride has only a slight chance of actually killing the hippo, that too only if it is very strategic. But the chances are very low. In case the lion pride meets the hippo close to the water, then the lion pride doesn't stand a chance. On the other hand, if they meet in the middle of the savannah, then the hippo doesn't stand a chance, as very soon all the UV rays from the Sun will be too much for the hippo to handle and then it will get weaker.

Fun fact- A group of hippos is called a pod!

RHINOCEROS

So as usual, most of you definitely know what a rhinoceros is, but for those who don't know, here is a quick introduction. A rhinoceros is a large mammal with a horn. Now for some interesting facts about it. It is the 2nd largest land mammal in the world. Even though it is herbivorous, it is extremely fierce and by fierce I don't mean that it is going to attack you whenever it sees you, but if you get close to its young ones, it will definitely charge at you. It perceives you as a threat and will stop chasing you only when it feels that you are no longer a threat to it or its young ones. Although they are big, they are not invincible. Animals like elephants and hippopotamuses can defeat the rhinoceros in a fight. The elephant can defeat the rhinoceros on land

and water whereas the hippopotamus will have an advantage in the water.

Fun fact- Rhinoceros have a special connection with tick birds. Rhinoceroses have lots of ticks on their bodies so the tick birds sit on the rhinoceros's back and eat the ticks! In return for the meal, the tick birds start looking out for predators and when they see one, they start to make loud chirping sounds to warm the rhinoceroses about the upcoming danger.

Elephants

Elephants are very common so most of you know about them. But some people might not. So we will do a quick introduction. Elephants are large eared, large trunked, large tusked mammals! Elephants are the largest land mammals that ever lived. Its ivory tusks are wanted across the world as display items they are very expensive. For this reason, humans poach elephants. You might have realised that when we talked about all the other animals, there is a mention of the elephant in most of them.

Fun Fact- Did you know what female elephants stay around their babies separated from the male elephants? The male elephants are also bigger than the females.

Fun Fact No. 2- African elephants are bigger and weigh more than the Asian elephants. The African elephant's ear almost resembles the shape of the African continent!!

Let's now travel to the next destination. get your snow cap and sweater, it is going to be cold...

Antarctic and Arctic Region

We have finished with the African Savannah. Now we shall see what animals inhabit Antarctica and the Arctic region. First we go with Antarctica.

Blue Whale

Blue Whales are the largest living water animal. Coming at a 100 feet long, these behemoths have no predator. Even though these large aquatic mammals are herbivores, they are too big for any other ocean predator to hunt and kill them. About twenty orcas could kill a juvenile blue whale but the chances of them killing an adult blue whale is zero. So for this reason, the blue whale is considered as an invincible species.

Fun fact: Blue whales might be the largest living animals to exist on planet earth, but it is not the largest living organism to exist on planet earth.

Some trees could be bigger than a blue whale. A huge cluster of fungus connected by roots will be counted as a living organism and it is bigger than the blue whale.

Penguin

At first glance, you might think penguins are a very simple species. But there is far more to the penguins than you think. The emperor penguin, has got its name for a reason. It's because, it can reach up to the average adult's leg. Penguins are known to lie on their stomach and slide across the ice to get to places faster, as penguins walk very slowly. Penguins are smarter than you think. To avoid getting eaten by predators inside the water, the penguins rush to the surface. They move faster on land than most of their predators do, as the predators are all aquatic. Even though the penguin's walk may be very slow when compared to the humans, they are definitely faster than most of their predators. Most of you think penguins as herbivores, but the truth is they eat fish by diving into the water. This is the time when leopard seals and orcas try to eat the penguins.

Fun fact: Did you know, that even the penguin's predators have predators? For example, predators such as leopard seals do get attacked by orcas.

ORCAS

Orcas are a member of the dolphin family. Some call them killer whales but they are quite gentle to people. Orcas are not only found in the Antarctic, but also in other places too. I know this is hard to believe, but in other regions, orcas are known to eat sharks to protect their young ones. Great white sharks will attack a young orca if the mother or the father is not around to guard it. But in the Antarctic, orcas mainly feed on penguins and other smaller animals that are present in the waters. A group of orcas is also called a pod-similar to the hippos which we discussed about earlier in the African Savannah. In the non- Antarctic waters, orcas eat squid by tearing off the squid's tentacles. But they will only do this if their young ones are in danger from the squid.

Fun fact: I have already mentioned this before when we were talking about the blue whales. It takes about 20 orcas to kill a juvenile blue whale.

Now we will talk about the animals in the Arctic region.

Polar Bear

Most of you know what a polar bear is. But for the people who don't know, the polar bears are large and powerful creatures. They hunt mostly walruses and any other animal they feel are delicious! Polar bears usually attack walruses on land because despite the fact that they are great swimmers, the walrus's body is built for moving under water so the polar bear doesn't stand a chance if it attacks them in the water. That's why it prefers to capture walruses before it moves into the water. If the polar bear goes into water, it will simply be dragged under water by the walruses. So polar bears rule the land and walruses rule the sea!

WALRUS

Some of you know about the walrus and some don't. So for the people who don't, walruses have long tusks and funny faces! Walruses eat clams.

When they search through the water for clams, their head clears all the dirt on the ocean's floor. When they find the clams, they keep their mouth at the clam's shell and quickly take back their tongue to create a vacuum and suck the tasty chewy part of the clam. They use the two fins on their back to propel them forward while the fins on the side help them steer through the ice.

Fun fact: If the walrus goes inside the water and if the sheet of ice covers the surface, then the walrus will use its head to break the ice and come up to the surface so that it can breathe.

Arctic Wolf

Arctic wolves are very similar to other wolves, except that their fur is white and they tend to have smaller packs. Like other wolves, they hunt in a pack. The co-ordinate with each other to take on large prey. they don't use the same hunting style as their relatives, as in the other wolves take on solitary animals whereas in the arctic, the arctic wolves have no other choice but to go after musk ox which roam around large herds. Once wolf a pack spots the musk ox, they go for the young ones. But this will not be easy for the white wolves as the musk ox will keep the young ones inside a circular formation of musk ox and won't let the arctic wolves pass through. Some hunts are a failure and some are successful. Even if you are an apex predator (predators who don't have any competition from other predators), the prey defends itself fiercely and even the arctic wolves might not succeed all the time. But when they are not able to kill musk ox, they go for other smaller prey in the arctic.

Musk Ox

Most of you might not know about musk ox. So I'll just quickly introduce the musk ox. Musk Oxen are large and strong. They have a coat that covers them and they have horns on their head. They often fight against each other. Just like in the Africa Savannah with the zebra, if the intruder comes into the herd, the musk oxen fight with each other for dominance. The one that is stronger will chase the other one out of the herd. One important fact, musk oxen uses their powerful horns to attack the enemy. So, think of bison. Have you seen them fighting? Just like that the musk oxen ram into each other with their heads. Also, there is a protective layer inside the skin that protects their brain from any injury so that the musk ox does not get hurt during a battle. I might have mentioned this before, musk oxen defend themselves from arctic wolves and ram the arctic wolf that gets too near their young ones. They will defend themselves from any upcoming threat. In summer time, the Arctic looks nothing like how it looks in the other seasons. There are plants, trees and there is plenty of grass. In the winter season, the musk ox eats the left over grass from the summer season.

You might want to get some boots and a lot of mosquito spray for this journey to......

SWAMP

Now that we have finished with Antarctica and Arctic region, we shall move on to the swamps. Swamps are covered with water. They are dark and they are filled with mosquitoes, alligators and dragon flies.

Mosquito

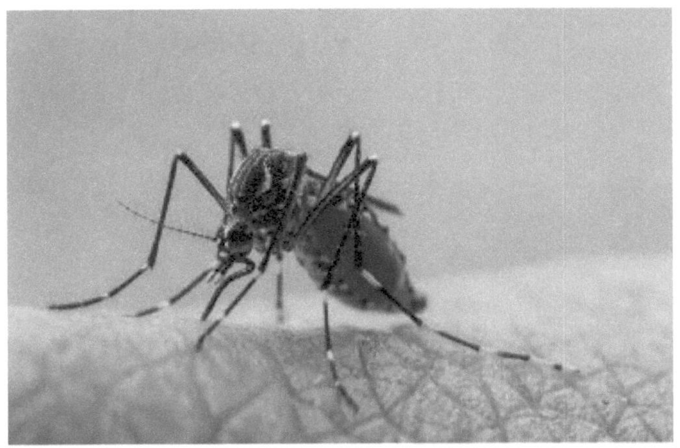

Every single one of you will definitely know what mosquitoes are. Most of you might not know this, that it is only the female mosquitoes that bite us. The male mosquitoes drink nectar from flowers. Blood contains Vitamin D and protein which are needed for the female mosquito to lay her eggs. So in a way she is encasing her larvae inside the blood There are millions of species of mosquitoes but only a hundred species bite humans. The other Ninety-nine thousand nine hundred species feed on other types of food such as nectar like other insects do. Mosquitoes can sense heat from our breath. When we breathe, hot air is expelled.

The mosquitoes are able to detect this heat and are able to find us.

Fun fact: A group of mosquitoes is called a swarm.

ALLIGATOR

Alligators have long, U-shaped snouts. Their teeth are curved inside their mouth. They are smaller than crocodiles but still they are aggressive. They are greyish in colour. Alligators sometimes attack cougars (cougars are wild cats). Adult cougars and adult alligators will fight most of the times for food. Alligators will sometimes attack young cougars while cougars will sometimes attack young alligators. Alligators ambush their prey, as in, they hide and attack. Alligators wait patiently in the water waiting for prey to arrive for a drink. Just when the prey arrives, the alligator will strike. Sometimes, it is successful and at other times, they prey escapes.

Dragon Fly

When dragon flies are born, they appear strange, like aliens. They are green in colour, and they look nothing like the ones we see in our neighbourhood. They will have big eyes and long legs. They have sharp looking jaws. The dragon fly larvae live under water and eat mosquito eggs. They swim very fast. Compared to an average sized human, the dragon fly's larvae have no chance to outswim them, but compared to critters such as a mosquito, they are fast. Then when it is going to reach adult stage, its head pops out of the green exoskeleton, then its entire body emerges. It sits down and rests its wings for some time, giving them the time to get ready for its first flight.

Fun fact: Dragon flies eat mosquitoes.

Get an oxygen tank and a diving suit if you want to survive......

OCEAN

Bass

We are going to talk about bass that live in ponds and lakes as there is no difference except for a thinner body. There are two types of bass. The large-mouth bass and the small-mouth bass. Small mouth bass eat shrimp. Large-mouth bass eat sunfish. Small-mouth bass live in groups while large-mouth bass live alone. Large- mouth bass need to protect their eggs from sunfish. They have nesting places called spawning grounds. Large-mouth bass are big while small mouth bass are a small fish.

Mako Shark

Mako sharks are fast, really fast. Their main prey consists of sword fish. They are one of the most dangerous Sharks in the world.

SALT WATER CROCODILES

Salt water crocodiles are the biggest types of crocodiles in the world making them one of the biggest reptiles in the world. They eat fish. Compared to alligators, they are longer and have a V-shaped snout. They are greenish and their teeth stick out of the mouth. Its relative the Nile crocodile, is one of the most dangerous animals in Africa. They lay their eggs and bury them. They guard their eggs day and night with occasional breaks to go cool down in a nearby pond. Once the eggs have hatched, the crocodiles take them with its teeth gently drops them into the water until they are old enough. Till then they guard them from predators.

Fun fact: All crocodiles, alligators, caiman are part of the family - Crocodilian!

FROG FISH

Sounds strange right? Well, believe it or not, something like that exists. It is a rounded frog headed, frog legged creature with strange protrusions on its back that match the coral reefs. In fact, this is no accident as the frog fish has the ability to change colour. This tactic is A) used to avert predators and B) used to catch prey. When fishes come too near, the frog fish snaps its mouth shut. It can actually do this in 0.1 seconds! Overall, these attributes help the frog fish become a successful predator and not become prey for other creatures. This is actually a major advantage in the animal kingdom as most predators need to make themselves visible to land a strike. But since the frog fish can launch its tongue out and grab the animal within a few milliseconds, any nearby predator would not have time to notice it.

POLYP

Now, polyps are certainly a creature that not many people have heard about as it is very hard to find and only comes out at night. I'll tell you why, Polyps are attached to the coral reefs that are a part of their defence.

This gives them protection against predators much like the frog fish. This is very important to a polyp as it is only an inch long. It has a harpoon like structure that allows it to catch shrimp which are smaller than they might seem. The polyp is a successful creature which does not need much help as it has protection and a plentiful food source. But, some fish species have included polyps in their diet. For this reason, the frog fish is needed. As I said before, the frog fish is able to disguise itself as coral reefs and inside coral reefs are polyps. When a fish comes too near, the frog fish snaps shut. This is known as a symbiotic relationship- (relationship in which 2 animals benefit from each other).

Remora and Great White Shark

The remora has an eel like body, but one thing it does not have in common with all eels is that it can attach itself to other creatures using suction (by creating a vacuum) and attracting itself to the creature. It's more common choice are great white sharks and manta rays. This gives it protection as very few creatures are powerful or brave enough to tackle a great white shark. The remora also gets plenty of food as when the great white shark bites down on some unwary sea creature, some of the skin and flesh floats away from the shark. This is what the remora eats.

Giant Squid

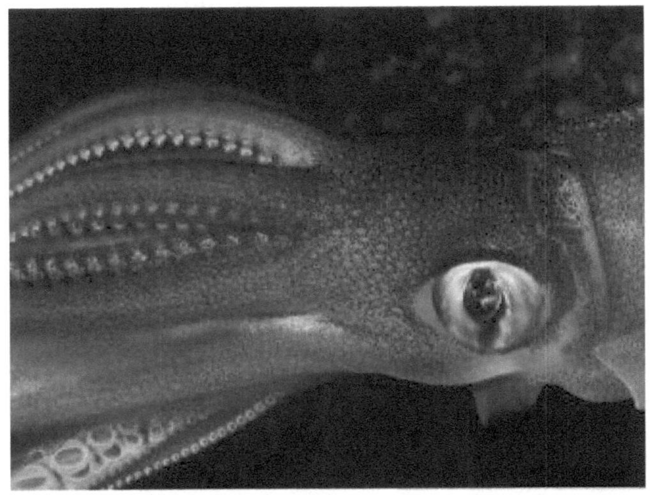

Giant squids have eyes as big as a soccer ball! They also have a beak in the middle of their tentacles. Now is a great time to clear out a common misunderstanding. *All of the squid's tentacles are not tentacles!!!* The two large ones on the side are known as arms and the rest are tentacles. Squids are also very powerful creatures and easily dominate the food chain as their only competition are the sperm whales and orcas. This is mostly because of the fact that the squid's skin is soft and stretchy like rubber, so you cannot pull off limbs from this creature! Biting will also be of little use, as their rubbery texture can withstand huge wear and tear. So the only real way to defeat a giant squid is to get in your mouth. This is also not very easy as while the tentacles are pretty easy to get inside your mouth, the giants arms will be wrapped around your body, stretching itself so that it can get out of your mouth. It also has serrated sharp patterns on its arms and tentacles. Meaning, it also has one of the strongest grips in the world. This is actually a huge contrast to its slimy and stretchy skin.

Clown Fish

Sounds funny, right? Well like Marlin says, clown fish are not as funny as other fish. As in, not at all! But jokes aside they are fascinating creatures. The fathers go out to eat food and bring food for the young ones. As you know, clown fish live is sea anemone giving protection against predators. A Sea anemone is an underwater plant that has a toxic venom that if touched, can cause serious problems to your body.

This is similar to the jelly fish which has a toxic chemical in its tentacles. Clown fish gradually develop immunity to the sea anemone's venom. When they are born, they have some basic immunity to the venom in their genes. But, after this they need to nurture this ability further by getting stung by the anemone a few times. Just like you can't get used to hot water without bathing in it for a few days, you can't get used to the venom without being stung a few times!

> *Fun fact: If a female clown fish dies after giving birth to offspring, the male will gradually change into a female. The first part of the body that will be affected is their brain. They will start feeling the urge to protect their young as fiercely as possible. What is even more surprising is that, the offspring will then become the male, mating with his now female parent!!!*

Blue Tang

Blue tangs, believe it or not, are the species the character Dory belongs to from Finding Nemo. They are actually highly venomous creatures so that already makes them fierce. But they also have the ability to shove their tail bone and fin bone out of their flesh and skin to fight predators! Also, blue tangs have very impressive memory. One of the best among fish!

Sockeye Salmon

Sockeye Salmon are a group of fish known for A) their ability to jump and B) social capabilities. It's a common misunderstanding, that fish are dumb and don't understanding anything about social relationships. This is deciphered from the fact that some fish don't live in groups. Well, everyone knows that a group of fish in general is called a school. But most people think that these groups can only contain 20-30 members. But the truth is, a school of fish can even contain a 100 members. This is especially true for the sockeye salmon as alone, they are quite helpless falling prey to river otters, eagles and black bears. But when they are in schools they look like one large creature. This is done because of a special ability called swimmer sense. Swimmer sense is when two fish can share brains!! This ability can be turned on and off so it doesn't affect them negatively. Because of this swimmer sense, they are able to turn in the same direction and move in the same speed and look like one large unified creature. For those who are wondering how can black bears live in the ocean, I'll tell you, they can't. Most of the sockeye salmon's life is in the ocean. But when it's time to deliver offspring, they swim to the river. This is the time predators I mentioned here try to get them.

OCTOPUS

An octopus is a cephalopod, same as the giant squid. Just that, the octopus is much better! I will tell you why. Although squids are well, giant, the octopus has some unknown abilities that make them such a successful creature. First comes their intelligence. Most cephalopods and animals in general are thought to be very stupid. But this is untrue especially for the octopus. It has the ability to use tools. While it does have a beak like the giant squid, it's not hard enough to say, crack a clam and get to the nice chewy inside. So the octopuses get creative. They take a nearby rock which looks strong, to break the clam open. This along with the fact that they have eight arms, means that they can handle multiple tools at the same time giving them an advantage over most animals in the sea.

This is because they have a large clump of neurons in each of their appendages which act as secondary brains, meaning each appendage can think for itself.

An unknown ability of the octopus is the ink- blast ability where it shoots a poisonous liquid into the water which is strong enough to kill a shark! Another ability is its arm regeneration. How does it do this? Well, its brain tells its body to keep making twin cells. This means a cell can genetically reproduce and create a daughter cell which can have twin cells. This can go on till a number of copies are produced. Using this method, they can regenerate a missing body part. This is a very similar tactic to what a salamander uses. Yet another ability of the octopus is its jet propulsion. On its head, next to its arms are two tiny holes which are visible to the naked eye. These holes have muscles which pull in water and release them at such a fast pace, that its able to thrust itself away from approaching threat or towards prey. Overall, it is a creature which such tremendous abilities that it is able to rest itself in a comfortable position in the food chain. Wait, what? I missed a point? Yes, friends, the octopus has the ability to camouflage itself into its surroundings. The colour it uses most frequently is grey, as it lives deep inside the water and most rocks there are grey in colour. Not only this, but it can change the texture of its body. This means, not only can it look like a rock, it can also feel like a rock.

Sword Fish

Sounds like a fish from a cartoon series right? But in fact the sword fish is real and just like name, it has a sword on its face! Some species of sword fish don't have a reason for developing these protrusions on their face. But some such as the actual sword fish, do. Sword fish is actually a family in which there is a species known as sword fish. There are also other fishes in the sword fish family. For the sword fish this reason for having protrusions is hunting. Reaching and attacking objects from a distance is safer than going near to bite it. This is a very useful tactic which some animals use. Another member of the sword fish family is the marlin. It is one of the fastest creatures on the planet- in fourth place!!!This is because of its streamlined body.

This helps it avoid the water resistance. If you don't know about aerodynamics, here is a quick intro. Animals with a flatter body can travel faster as there are less air molecules or water molecules they are hitting.

Get lots of water it's going to be hot...

DESERT

Gila Monster

Gila monsters have strong jaws they use to battle other Gila monsters. Their bites are poisonous and their backs are very slippery. They have claws which they use to fight cats and also try to take on other Gila monsters. The bites are extremely strong.

Rattle Snake

The rattle snake is a formidable threat to any animal smaller than an elephant, unless the animal has immunity to venom. There is a confusion between the terms poison and venom, while poison is a harmful substance that you eat or drink, venom is something that is injected into your bloodstream. Snakes sink their fangs into your arm/ leg so they release venom, but how does venom work? Well once it enters your bloodstream, it can do a number of things depending on what type of venom it is. For snakes it enters the nerves (long wires that send signals from the brain to organs and body parts like the fingers you are using to turn the page) and the venom molecules get lodged in them stopping the signals from reaching, stopping your heart, lungs etc.

What Is Anti- Venom?

Anti-venom is of course the cure for venom. But how does it work? Well it has to do with the vaccine. The reason we put vaccines is because the vaccine itself has a weak version of the virus mixed into it, this makes the immune system create a chemical to combat the weak virus and if the actual disease infects you it will deploy the chemical. So doctors put snake venom inside a cow take chemical that fought the venom and inject it into a human.

We're going to travel back in time to see the strangest things.....

Strange Facts and Distant Cousins

SNAKES AND CROCODILES

We all have shivers sent down our spines when we see either of these creatures. But what you might not know, is that they were sending shivers down each other's spines ever since their species came into existence.

Titanoboa was a large 50 feet extinct snake with curved teeth and the appearance of a boa and behaviour of an anaconda. It didn't move that fast on land, but in water it was agile and swift. It fed on fish and other small aquatic animals.

On the other hand, a giant 20 – 25 feet crocodile, swam the earth at the same time as the titanoboa.

Although the size difference is huge, this pre-historic crocodile was fierce competition to the titanoboa. Its dietary preferences were fish and small aquatic animals, the same as the titanoboa. Due to this, the titanoboa and the prehistoric crocodile were enemies.

The jaw of the crocodile could have proved to be an advantage in a fight. If it was able to bite the snake strong enough, it could win. This can only happen if it is not constricted by the titanoboa, meaning squeezed to death until the prey cannot breathe anymore. The titanoboa slowly lost the battle due to the competition in food and the climate change and became extinct.

Just because titanoboa became extinct, it doesn't mean that the rivalry between snakes and crocodiles is over. Even in modern times, they have the instinct that they are enemies. For example, there have been several instances where dead crocodiles have been found inside the stomach of dead anacondas and other huge snakes. In other instances, small snakes attack an average sized crocodile or alligator and get eaten. But unlike the titanoboa, these snakes spread all across the world. Since crocodiles and alligators were the only animals that can fight against these snakes and their relatives, it didn't look good for the crocodilian family as they had failed in stopping the snakes from spreading all over the world. Snakes thus technically win the war.

CROCODILES AND ELEPHANTS

Unlike the war between the crocodiles and the snakes, this isn't an evolutionary war. In fact, it's not a war at all, it's more like rivalry between two species.

Crocodiles don't often choose to attack the elephants. They just see the trunk and mistake it for something very weak and have no idea that there is an elephant. If a crocodile grabs an elephant's trunk, mostly the elephant would swing the trunk around like a mad animal until the crocodile has either given up or is dead. Also, due to the elephant's memory, they are able to recall incidents that happened in their childhood. They also feel emotions like humans and would remember the death of their relatives even if it was many years back. So an elephant could remember that a crocodile attacked one of its relatives and will attack it of it sees it again in its lifetime.

Furthermore, the elephants are not only known to kill the murderers of their dear ones, but also to hang them on trees. For example, a dead crocodile was seen to be put on a tree by an adult elephant in Africa!

Crocodiles are known to climb trees although not evolutionarily equipped to do so. This could explain a very mysterious discovery of a crocodile skeleton being found on the top of a tree! Even stranger- a herd of elephants are known to dwell in caves and eat rocks which sounds very strange, but the rocks are actually made out of salt. The elephants just break off these rocks and eat them! All these are strange facts, but more of these will follow.

It is well known in the animal kingdom that you should never grab an elephant by its trunk as it will simply whirl you around or keep thrashing the trunk here and there till animal is dead. But somehow, crocodiles are always known to target the trunk. More surprising, the crocodile is not stupid at all, it has the average intelligence of animals. But there's a reason the crocodiles target the trunk. Without their trunks, elephants cannot do most of the things they usually do. Some elephants can live without their trunks. If their trunk was bitten off by a predator or wounded severely, it will not pose a huge threat to the elephant as it would still look imposing. But for baby elephants, there is a chance that they may get into adulthood without their fully grown trunk.

Owls and Eagles

Owls and eagles have been natural enemies. Before the eagle species came, owls were thriving. After the eagles came, the owls had major competition. Owls and eagles are known to stack each other. This goes well for neither of them. Sometimes, the owl's flight and keen eyes would be too much for the eagle. In other circumstances, the eagle's talons and its speed would simply destroy the owl. Either way you put it, they are formidable enemies. Owls have the advantage at night. Due to their night vision, they are able to attack eagles without much difficulty. The eagle's lack of night vision could prove fatal or at least inflict hard blows. There have been many instances where owls have attacked eagles in the night and have won. They simply cannot tolerate each other!

If you go by size, you might think that's absolutely impossible. But owls have the ability to turn their heads 100 degrees to scan the surrounding areas. They are all over the world whereas eagles live only near mountains. Furthermore, it has been discovered by some scientists that ancient owls actually had talons. In modern day times, they have lost this feature. This could be perhaps because of some changes which made them less dependent on their legs or just a random mutation. It is really not that simple to just say that eagles and owls are evenly matched. Scientists have to dig deep into their confrontations to see which bird wins the mist often. Only then can they arrive at a conclusion as to which bird is superior.

Some people in zoos make the mistake of putting eagles and owls in the same enclosure. An incident like this happened where the officials found a dead eagle with an owl standing beside it. So wherever there are eagles, the zoo keepers make sure that the enclosure surrounding is owl free. Owls can see from great distances and so can eagles. If you zoom in on everything they do, they don't seem that different. One thing the owl and eagle don't have in common is that eagles actually use fire. Once, a fire fighter was called to put out a fire in a wild life sanctuary. Once he put it out, he saw eagles carrying sticks that were lit up and throwing them on the ground. This caused the fire. They did this because if you are prey running from the fire, you wouldn't care to check around for predators. The eagles use this tactic to attack animals in the confusion.

Continuing in the time traveller we're going to see how humans destroyed Australia.........

Australia

History and a quick introduction: Australia contained one of the largest variety of flora and fauna in the entire world. In today's time, Australia is mainly ruled by marsupials, whereas in ancient times, it had many other strange and interesting creatures such as the 16 feet komodo dragon or the massive giant ground sloths. These creatures existed about 15 million years ago. One of the deadliest predators were the big birds of the time. This was a mid-way point in the evolution from dinosaurs to birds we are familiar with as its sheer size and power was enough to make any man tremble with fear. With their large and powerful beaks, they can break effortlessly through armour and crack skulls. Moreover, their giant feet allowed them to topple over large mammals. But one of the most famous creatures of the time were Diprotodons- A large marsupial, with brown fur and large teeth. A larger version of the well-known beaver. These giant creatures were one of the main influencers of that era. For their size and sheer power allowed them to become one of the top species in Australia. It also made hunting them very hard.

EXTINCTION OF AUSTRALIAN MEGAFAUNA

After humans gained enough intelligence to build boats craft and customize their choice of weaponry, they first conquered Europe. Then they travelled eastwards towards Australia. This was perhaps the most monumental phase in human history. As this was the first time the human had ever set foot in Australia. But there was one problem - the local wildlife was not designed to cope with humans, resulting in a killing spree that wiped out half of the fauna in Australia. Ground sloths Diprotodons and the largest of the komodo dragons and all the other pre historic creatures started dying out due to the lack of members. This is due to the fact that Diprotodons don't know that humans are a threat. That mean they did not have the instinct to run away from us. The same thing happened to all the other Australian mega fauna alive and plenty of smaller creatures too. This resulted in the extinction of these beautiful creatures. Australia has indeed suffered a great loss. But it is continuing to be filled with creatures like kangaroos. know I would like to talk a bit about kangaroos – kangaroos are more dangerous than you think. their front arms have claws used for scratching other male kangaroos. (Just like with hippopotamus, these fights occur due to one challenging the other to a fight to lead group). This, along with their massive legs inflict major damage to anyone without a hard outer covering or a robust body. They are boxing champions. Just that instead of their arms, they box with their legs. These kicks, can send a person flying. Here's a story showing how terrifying they are. A few Australian residents suffered great loss when a mob of kangaroos kept on chasing and beating them up. After being badly boxed, they gave an interview and described whole thing.

Fun fact: Did you know girl kangaroos are known as Joeys and that they are faint blue in colour. Also, they are the only ones with pouches.

Note - I hope this short essay raised awareness of the damaging effects of human intervention in the green world we live in. Now keep in mind our ancestors did not know that hunting would lead to the extinction of these creatures but we do. So let us help save modern day animals by following these three rules:

1. Plant trees. One of the main reasons for the extinction of these animals was deforestation.

2. Contribute to any fundraisers relating to nature.

3. tell others.

In this next destination we're going to rest in a bench
and see what animals turn up.......

CITY

CORVIDS

All of you in this entire world know what a crow is. But the intelligence of crows is something less well known. You see, if you want to live in the city and you're not a human, you need to be small, nocturnal, smart and adaptable. The crow fits all these categories except nocturnal. Crows are very intelligent because they have to get though a number of obstacles in a very short amount of time. These obstacles are mainly pigeons and kite birds. A crow eats pigeon eggs. This is what they do. They have to strategically plan out every single move they make. They mostly try at night at about 8 to 9 pm. This is the time when their black body is least visible in the blurry night sky. They then use their ability to remember certain objects and patterns to carefully navigate the way through to the nest. After this they very silently fly away into the night sky. This is executed perfectly and needs a lot of communication between the crows. They have to make sure that it is perfectly safe to go to the pigeon's nest. So most of the time, they create a distraction leading the pigeon away from their nest. Furthermore, crows are also known to use tools. A few crows in the wild were spotted using sticks and play fighting. Much like human kids use things like pencils to childishly pay with each other. The adult crows are also seen using this strategy. They have been seen using rocks. In fact, one time, in about 1975, a group of crows started to pick up stones and then throw them from the sky. The first time they did this, it almost hit a construction worker and a car. Crows are also seen using fishing rods. No kidding! They actually peel a bit of bark from a small stick, put it into the water and go fishing. They have been seen doing this in cold places like Iceland and Greenland. This is not unique to crows. Even ravens have been spotted doing this. In fact, it's a common trait amongst the whole Corvid family. This, with their physical abilities make them one of the smartest and best city builds of all times.

Now we will be talking about another member of the corvid family, the raven:

The raven is an extremely intelligent animal. This has a lot to do with its genetic relation to the crow so they share many similarities. But the raven has a slightly bluer colour, a thicker and more robust body, a larger beak and in general and a more well-rounded body structure. The raven has the skills of a parrot. As in, it can not only make certain high pitched sounds like the crow, it can also mimic the voices of people or certain sounds from day to day life like the school bell, the honking of cars, opening and closing of a draw, the turning pages of a book the toilet flushing or the door bell ringing!! It uses these very clever tactics to trick humans into doing what it pleases. For eg. It could sit outside someone's window and make the sound of a doorbell ringing. Then once they have gone to check the door, it can quickly come inside and steal some food or in rare cases, jewellery or household appliances to trade with people to get food. The corvid family are no stranger to the word trade! On many occasions, they would pick up a pattern from certain incidents. Like maybe person giving out food because it accidentally dropped some pieces of gold that it found lying around on the road. Registering the information that if it brought certain items then it would get rewarded, it would bring back more of these items. Ravens also use objects to attack people. An example has been given in the 'crows' section. Ravens also have another incredible ability- and this is to learn from other ravens and even humans. What I mean is, they can remember from certain incidents if a human is a friend or a foe. For example, if a raven sat on your window, and then you chased it away, the negative incident with you would cause the raven to register you as a foe. But if you show it the face of a person it does not recognize, then it will rely on the reaction of its peers (fellow ravens or humans). In a similar way, ravens can observe a person executing a certain activity and then mirror that activity when the person is not watching. For eg. Let's say someone is going fishing and then the raven sees them. If they go take a break, there is a high probability it will also fish with its beak. There is one last ability of the raven that I just have to mention. That is the ability to form cross species co-operation in a beautifully executed symbiotic relationship such as howling like a wolf, to lead the wolves to a restaurant near the forest. Then in all the chaos it can grab itself a piece of food.

Fun fact: There is a castle in England where it is said that at least seven crows should reside for the castle to stay strong. This is due to the fact that crows played a role in the history of the castle.

Rat and Mice

Really does bring up the Tom and Jerry vibes doesn't it? Well, Jerry is actually a mouse. Most of you may be wondering what is the difference between rat and mice. Well, rats are bigger and have a greyish colour. Mice are smaller and have a brownish colour. They mainly feed on things like cheese. This is a very nice time to clear out a common misunderstanding. You see, the link between mice and cheese actually started when people put a high quality cheese (Swiss cheese) in the bottom shelf. This allowed mice to easily access this food and continuously target the cheese. This lead to the speculation that cheese is mice's general diet. But this is absolutely wrong. Because, in most of the places mice live, there's only greenery and vegetation.

So remember, the next time you hear that mice love cheese, remember, it's not in the way you think.

So anyway, mice are highly vulnerable to cats as they mostly choose to live in human houses. Perhaps not in the inside, they might live in the exterior part of the walls. They also live in places like basements and lobbies.

Now for Rats

Unlike mice, rats are not vulnerable to cats like you think. Of course, the cat will definitely eat the rat if it chooses, but this big member of the vermin family is too big and fierce to be on the cat's normal diet. Unlike mice, rats are much harder to catch or poison as they are bigger. Furthermore, they are ready to get into confrontation with a fierce predator. But they generally try to avoid humans. Rats are also extremely ferocious to each other – running, jumping and disrupting the whole environment. Not to mention chewing and thieving!

FALCONS AND PIGEONS

What are falcons? You may ask. Falcon is a huge predatory raptor. Oh no no no.. not the Dinosaur Raptor! Raptors are actually a species of bird family known for their sharp beaks, large talons and huge size. Anyway, falcons live in the African Savannah, the prairie and in the city. You may be wondering why I paired them with the pigeon. This imaginary scenario will show you why.

A falcon is sitting on a street lamp, scanning the area for any sight of prey. It sees a pigeon on a building. It flies up and then dives towards the pigeon. This way it can reach speeds of up to 75 miles per hour. It extends out its talons. Suddenly the pigeon notices this large lunging figure and decides to move away. But the falcon picks up so much speed that it has to wait till the end of the dive to resume the pursuit of the pigeon. It then starts flying at maximum speed. But the pigeon's small body is better for going through benches and street lamps. Eventually the falcon catches the pigeon. But if this does not happen, the pigeon will eventually find shelter as home, because they have a special ability known as homing. It can detect the correct ways to turn, even though it has never flown from this place to its home.

Dogs

Dogs are in parks, on roads, in highways, in short everywhere. They have been the most loved companions of humans since the time we started to become a dominant species, This is the reason the saying *"dog is a man's best friend"* came about. As most of you know, there are hundreds and even thousands of dog breeds each with its own characteristics. Here we will talk about the ones that are useful for things like protection, herding and search and rescue. Starting off with the king of those three tasks- the husky. Huskies are energetic, friendly and powerful dogs. They have a great sense of smell and are amazing at rounding up cattle. In fact, this is where they shine. Their thick coat helps them stay warm, perfect for tracking sheep in the snow this is the leading fact that makes huskies such a beast in search and rescue operations. Huskies are also good for tracking down animals for modern and olden time hunters. It's keen sense of smell can also detect predators and correctly warn the human. The husky's first course of action will of course be to run with its owner. But, if there is any instance where it has to fight back against a predator, it won't be shy.

Now, there are actually dogs specifically suited for fighting predators like bears. In fact, there is a dog specifically bred for this purpose. Meet the Bear Dog!

This is a type of dog that is built for fighting, oh sorry, dealing with bears. Notice how I said 'dealing'. In fact, it's the bears stupidity that even gives the bear dog a chance. You see, bear dogs are very brave. But they don't have any powerful muscles that can fight a bear. This is because it does not have to. Bears are an apex predator that chase other creatures and every time, these creatures run away and the bear chases after them. So when meeting a creature that without provocation starts chasing it, the bear's only response is to run as its mind hasn't been trained to deal with charging creatures. But if that particular bear is smart enough to see through the dog's acting, it and its owner would be in hot water!

Doberman are on the less family friendly side of things as there have been many cases of attacks. So it is advised to be a bit careful if the Doberman is not at all known. These dogs rub shoulder to shoulder with pit bulls and huskies as one of the strongest dog breeds. Doberman are better as pets for people who live alone than for families if they have not been accustomed to children and other dogs. They are better suited for people who like a source of protection. If any unwanted guests show up, a Doberman would be the best at protecting its owner.

House Cats

Cats are amazing in many ways and are under-appreciated by many and are looked at like a lazy animal with no purpose In your home. Dogs are showered with affection and are perceived as an entirely different thing that has no relation to cats but in reality they are quite similar! They are both in a group called the carnivorans (a group of mammals that have a special type of teeth that allows them to take in more protein from their prey). This group is divided into Feliformia and Califormia. Califormia use their heightened sense of smell to detect the carcass of an animal, they also have medium to high agility. The Feliformia have a high sense of sight and hearing thanks to their slit eyes. They also have speed and plus their muscular hind- legs that allow them to jump around with agility. This ability allows them to defend against larger animals using their arms to block upcoming strikes and counter- attack. Additionally, they can use their hind legs to jump out of that situation entirely. All of this is the reason cats were domesticated in the first place, as farmers needed a way to capture the insect eating their crops. Dogs can't jump high enough to catch them but cats can.

History

Cats are inquisitive, playful and energetic. Now would be a great time to clear up a common myth: cats are not lazy! The reason they sleep so often is that they roam around in the night! So they rest at day time. Anyways as I was saying: cats are inquisitive, playful and energetic creatures ....

History of cats: The cat family evolved from proailurus also known as" cat dog". As the name suggests it is a literal amalgamation of a cat and dog. This animal appeared in Africa and dominated the area at that time. Then it branched out into two animals. The cat lived in Africa but suddenly they started popping up in the place where the dogs lived, they had an advantage over the dogs. Which is hunting style: the hunting style of a cat perfectly matches with the skillset it possesses. Close your eyes, and imagine with me: the cat sneaks up on its prey from behind a bush... it gets as close as it can and then it pounces. The reason I call this perfect is because the cat's main assets is that it can move silently and attack fast.

But why do cats fight now? The reason is genetic memory (this theory states that memories of large scale events will be passed in the genome.)

Current cats and dogs literally have it in their genes to attack each other.

We have to do everything we can do to protect these creatures from ourselves

1. Leave them alone and don't go too close if they are not comfortable

2. Don't keep them in tight spaces

3. Don't breed them as they might not have strong genes and they might die

Get ready for never before seen life as this next destination contains animals that are nowhere else in the world

MADAGASCAR

Lemur Overview*

Almost all people reading this book know what a lemur is. But for the uninitiated, a lemur is a type of primate with a long snout, and flexible muscles. In fact, flexible muscles are one of the well-known attributes of a lemur. Their locomotion and control is so astonishing that not even monkeys can match up to it. But, in a sort of middle point of lemur's existence, monkeys started to grow fiercer and started becoming competition for the lemur. With the human uprising at its peak, lemurs became endangered. Also monkeys became fiercer as they needed to compete with apes for space. Not only homo sapiens but with homo neanderthals and all other homo species. So only the lemurs in the remote island of Madagascar survived and over there, began a golden age of lemur's existence. You see, before all lemurs were ginormous with massive proportions. But in Madagascar, the tree filled terrain changed them into small maneuverable creatures. Lemurs have thin webbed armpits. This webbing allows to catch air and fly like a parachute. Furthermore, they have great hand- eye co-ordination as the trees there have spikes and sharp thorns and these lemurs need to be extremely careful. Surprisingly, every time their hands fall right at the place with no spikes.

*I gave a brief overview in the start because this destination will mainly contain lemurs

AYE AYE

Sounds strange, doesn't it? It would sound even more strange if I told you that Aye Aye is related to woodpeckers. It would shock you even more if I tell you, it's also related to lemurs! Let me explain. An aye aye is genetically a lemur but from a behavioural standpoint it is more closely related to wood peckers. I'll break it down even more and explain it in even more detail. An aye aye uses sonar detection, as in it knocks on a hollow piece of wood. When it does this, a sound wave is created and flows through the log. Then the sound waves bounces back, meaning that it can sense a creature which is inside the log because the sound reflects on the creature and bounces back to the aye aye or wood pecker. So, this is how the aye aye does it. It has a big middle finger which is extra-long and bulky. When this finger taps it creates a reaction which leads to all that I just explained. Now for the lemur bit in the aye aye. The aye aye is genetically a lemur. It has the maneuverability and flexibility of a lemur. Also, it is the only mammal that makes nests like a bird, and especially on a tree.

Fun fact: An aye aye is actually considered unlucky by many people. Although untrue, this myth kept spreading and people started treating aye aye unfairly, as in chasing them away or hitting them with sticks.

Ring Tailed Lemur

Ring tailed lemurs are almost like normal lemurs but unlike normal lemurs, they fight for the female! But first, let me tell you the things that they have in common with other lemurs-The female always leads the group. She is the alpha female.

Now this is specifically interesting, since almost all primates make men their leader. For example, in chimpanzee groups, men are voted through social abilities whereas with gorillas, it depends on strength. Now, as for the gorillas the male is usually the strongest. All males that have a silver back are usually stronger than others. But females don't get this mark so it is definitely logical for men to be ones who are competing. But in the case of chimpanzees, females actually have more social capabilities than men. This is the reason women are the ones usually working together to take care of their babies. So in the case of chimpanzees it is unfair hierarchy. These systems are quite like humans because the stronger men, forbid the more social women to be treated the way they deserve. So, it is interesting to know that only lemurs have a female leader. Now, as per rules, the female gets to eat first and is usually treated with respect. Whereas new members to the group are to eat scraps and leftovers of its grand lemur counterparts like the female and the other senior males. There is one way for both males and females move up the rank which is what I mentioned earlier- fighting. Now their fighting is not what you would think. Here is a very interesting phenomena. Ring tailed lemurs act like human politicians. They rub their hands together and create a sort of pheromone which is like a message saying, "this is our turf, please stay out!". There is another gland which produces a very smelly pheromone which lemurs use as sort of a weapon. This is what they do, they rub their chest which is where the gland is present and then throw the smell on to their opponent. This is mainly used for attracting females. And also moving up ranks.

MOUSE LEMUR

Sounds strange right? Well, at first a mouse lemur might appear to be harmless, but the truth is, they are mini killing machines. They can fight leeches and cockroaches and flies. How? Well, they have sharp teeth and large eyes which allow them to see in very dark places. These creatures are also very very fat! This means they have more mass (For those who don't know, mass is the amount of atoms contained within an object and this is densely* packed. Meaning that it has a lot of weight. So, if it launches a strike at one of its opponents, its mass will be sure to crush them. Plus, the teeth, which makes them a good living insect repellent. They are also good in fighting cockroaches and leeches. The only other creature that I can think of which could beat the mouse lemur in open combat on the plains of Madagascar is the tenrec.

* Being tightly compressed inside an area.

Tenrec

Tenrecs, unlike their name, are neither big nor wrecks. The live all over the earth. In the water, over the tree tops, under the ground itself and on land. Now, we will start with the underground Tenrec. The underground Tenrec is much bigger than its counterparts as it is basically built for dozing through think layers of sand. It also does not have any eyes! This is because, the underground tunnels are so dark and humid that having eyes would be an unnecessary waste of resources. So, it has developed a big body plus a long tongue to easily grab any creature that might come into its path. For example, worms. As most of you know, worms are the primary diet of any burrowing creature as it is abundant all over the world and in mass quantities. It is also one of the only food that exists in the underground tunnels. So they need to have a wide variety of skills to capture their only food source.

We've looked underground, now we will look over the tree tops. This Tenrec climbs a lot like primates as it has a prehensile tail. A tail that acts much like a fifth limb, but is much more flexible and bendable. So anyway, as you can imagine, creatures travelling through tree tops need to be small, and this Tenrec is. So a prehensile tail like this helps the Tenrec move more flexibly. It can provide flexibility and strength that its other limbs do not have. This means, it can go quickly and carefully through the tree tops.

Now, we shall look inside the water. This Tenrec naturally has webbed feet. It also has, water proof fur which allows it to become dry in an instant. It relies mainly on the direction of the water. But, it can turn and twist very smoothly. It is much slower than the tree Tenrec, but is more controlled. It also lives is small burrows right next to the water so that in the small chance of a predator finding its home, it can easily slip away. Literally!

Now, for the most interesting Tenrec of the bunch. The land Tenrec! What makes it different from other Tenrecs is that it has a defense mechanism which is

– spikes. It has small spikes on its back that it can use to defend itself from predators. Now, these spikes are not only used for defense but also for offense! Now, let us say that Tenrec is going hunting. They usually eat small insects like cockroaches, mites, beetles and worms. This is due to the fact that they are too small to hunt any other life form, not because they done have the necessary resources to hunt bigger game. Anyway, let us say, a predator like a weasel were to discover the Tenrec and attack it. Tenrecs use their sharp spikes to fight against the much bigger predator. It does this by charging forward with its spikes bending forward. If it gets a good hit in any location like the eyes or nose, the weasel has a 99% chance of death. Perhaps, if it hits some place like the legs, it has 0% chance of death. Also, they can create an ultrasonic sound which is in the form of their spikes chattering. This ultrasonic sound helps locate their young. You see, there are a very few special types of animals whose eyes or ears are designed to see or hear things which other animals cannot. For example, the dragon fish can see a special type of bio-luminescent* in the ocean light that nobody else can.

*Bio luminescent light is when animals mix certain chemicals together to create a glow.

We are now going to arrive at the area where the amazon jungle is situated.......

AMERICA

The West African Honey Bees

Now, before I start talking, I'd just like to say, that West African honey bees were actually transported to America from Africa

Classes of Bees and Structure

Do you know what it would be like to go inside a bee colony? Well I do! So I'll tell you what will happen if you approach a bee colony and go inside it. Wait! First, I'll get out my shrink ray and shrink us to the size of a bee. But before we go in, don't forget to get some pollen or nectar. Why you ask? So once you approach the area, you'll see hundreds of guard bees who would be standing there on their hind legs and would chase away anything that didn't have their pheromone*. But if that other bee brings nectar, then the guards will offer a truce and let the bee deliver its gift! Yaay! We're in. Wait, do you see those bees dancing? Well, that's just another the way bees talk to each other when they want to tell the other bees that they found flowers. How fast they dance and wriggle, how much area they cover, all of this tells something about where the flower is. Hey! What's that little insect doing here? It doesn't have a stinger so it can't be a bee right? Guess what? This is a special type of bee called the drone bee. The only reason they are there is that one of them will marry the queen bee and once it's done that it's of no use. So if there's a famine or something, the drone bees will get kicked out of the colony.

Look at those hexagon patterns! Guess what's inside them? Well, bees store all sorts of things inside. Like pollen, nectar and even bee- larvae. Here's the shocking thing! Once a bee- larvae has hatched, in twenty days, it'll clean up the hexagon in which it was born and make it ready for the next bee to be born. So these are little storage shelves. Hey, but what's that over there? Why are all these bees lying down on leaves?

Well, this is actually a bee hospital! Sick bees stay here and worker bees bring them the finest nectar and even some medicinal herbs. Well, let's continue our journey. Oh no! is that a monster bee? No this is actually the queen bee! She's twice the size of a normal one! But she is actually the stupidest bee in the entire colony but none the less she has a pheromone that controls the other bees leaving her to be the queen. This type of team work is called eusociality

***Influence on the environment'**

This was done to increase livestock, but something got seriously out of hand. The West African honey bees started to escape from their enclosures and get out into the wild! They started spreading rapidly all around America. Now, the problem with these bees is that they don't pollinate. They use the nectar to make honey. Now, I know you're thinking, "So what if these bees don't pollinate? The other bees in America will do so!" The issue is West African honey bees are a lot fiercer and more competitive than other bees. So they began exterminating all the other bee species. Things got even worse when hornets dropped into America. The problem here is they broke into west African honey bee colonies and stole the honey. For some months they plundered through the hives but the in the most recent years, scientists have noticed that bees have developed a new tactic to defeat the hornet. They would pile around the hornet and stop its oxygen supply, thereby killing it. Now, this increased their ferocity and helped them to work as a team. Because of this, they've been killing countless insects and other bees. So, there are no other insects or other bees to pollinate the flowers. For now, everything is holding steady because of the hornets. But perhaps in the years to come, the West African honey bee might find a way to wipe hornets out of the map, then they will be unstoppable, killing creatures left and right! This will affect the human economy as well, as this means the West African honey bees will take all the honey for itself. So there will be a shortage of honey for humans and that means they can't sell as much as they used to. So unless you want a pandemonium, please pray that all the West African honey bees will be sent back to Africa. There they will evolve into calmer species as the wild life there is fit for them.

"*In the insect world, everyone talks using smells. Each smell has its own meaning. For eg: termites give off an irritating smell and this smell says, "keep away! Keep away!". Termites will also give off warning pheromones telling their friends to be cautious. Like this, there are also troop pheromones. What I mean is, each bee colony will have its own smell. So, if a bee that belongs to another bee colony try to penetrate this bee hive, the guard bees will shoo it away. So just to be clear, a pheromone is a scent that insects give off to tell things to each other or know who is who.

Pronghorn

A cheetah is the fastest land mammal right? Well in reality there is a creature that can run as fast as a cheetah but only has few of its disadvantage's*. This animal is the pronghorn. It is a relative of the giraffe but closely resembles a deer, anyways so a pronghorn is fast ok but it also has another perk which is its resilience. It can shrug of a few hits and it can also deliver some with it's horns. Although strictly speaking its horns are more for intimidation than actual action.

Scientific name: Antilocapra Americana

Speed: 95 kmph

Defect: the pronghorn can't jump.

Vampire Bat

Vampire bats are bats that drink blood. Now they are very similar to the ghost bat when it comes to size. The vampire bat is the only bat that drinks blood. It's also the only bat that can run or walk. It mainly drinks blood from large mammals like cows.

Bald Eagle

The Bald eagle lives in mountainous areas. This is because these places have very little trees so they will spot prey more easily. They have a surprising amount of different feathers. This applies for all birds in general. All feathers are like brush pens, as in, there are large bristles then shorter ones, that make up the larger ones, then on the tip of those, they have extremely small bristles. How many bristles there are will tell you what kind of feather it is.

For eg. If there are thick bristles and there are many of them then these are called downy feathers. These are used to keep young chicks warms. Now you might be wondering why are they called bald eagles if they have feathers from the time they are born. Well, it is because there is a large white patch on the bald eagle's head. This makes it look bald from afar. Then we have flight feathers: these have thin bristles that are light. These grow on the eagle when they are a bit older. The feathers are quite large and help catch air and help them look intimidating.

Now, let us talk a bit about their place in the food chain in its small territory in America. The bald eagle has very few threats. Even black bears don't dare to mess with these creatures. Their razor- sharp talons are enough to pierce any protective layer of skin or fur. It is a bit like being stabbed by broken glass. They use their dominance to catch large ducks that roam around in ponds.

Get a good knife, there are a lot vines in the next
destination.....

Amazon Jungle

Weaver Ant

Deep in the jungle is being fought a war by ants, such as the smart weaver ants. Weaver ants create castles using leaves. They are fierce protectors of their nests. They protect their eggs from army ants and all other types of ant species. They can shoot acid out of their bodies. They fight with their bare hands. Carpenter ants also try to attack their nests. Now let's see how weaver ants make their nests. Weaver ants are led by a major. This major is characterized by certain unique traits that make them perfect defending the workers. These majors fan out and find a leaf which has the correct amount of durability and flexibility. They then send out chemical pheromones (specialized chemical messages allowing them to communicate with one another.) to the workers. When this chemical is received loud and clear, the workers quickly hurry to the spot and pull the leaf from the branch. They then take it to the nest. Most of you may not know this, but weaver ant's larvae can produce a specialized silk thread useful for binding materials together. So, when the workers bring the leaf, they take the larvae to bind the leaves together. They make hundreds of nests like this. The Queen ant is always inside a big nest in the middle of these nests.

Argentine Ants

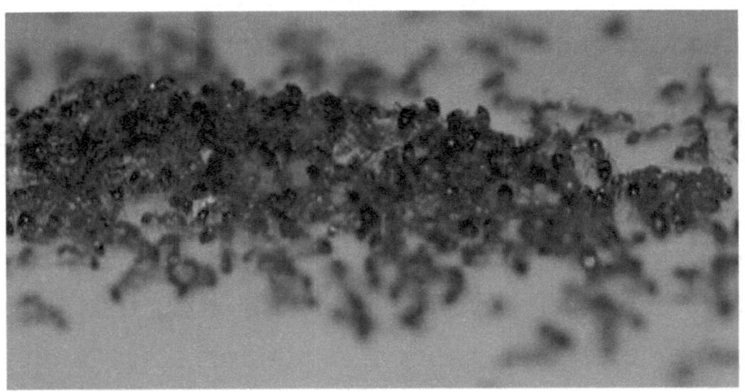

These type of ants make super colonies, thanks to humans! They were originally in swamps in North Argentina. These creatures were certainly the underlings because they were very small and did not possess any weapons that could help them in their struggles against the other ants. Other bigger ants like fire ants and army ants easily defeated them and ignored them. The problem with the argentine ants is that they are always in search of new territory. They always take some of their babies with them. You see, argentine ant Queens lay over 9000 eggs a day. So, after a few generations the genes slowly started to change from the original colonies*. So, they perceive the wandering part of their colony as another colony by itself resulting in unwanted conflicts. Argentine ants were nothing special until the humans came into play. They started to transport goods and food through ships to different locations around the world. A few argentine ant Queens got stuck in one of these ships causing them to land in a new environment where they faced not predators and only had prey. This allowed them to multiply but there is something great about this that leaves scientists stunned!

Since there are technically no enemies in these new locations, the argentine ant colonies are able to communicate very flexibly. In fact, this huge communication network does not only apply to only 2-3 colonies. But to the entire argentine ant species as a whole. They are so vast in number that even though they don't have any special capabilities such as poison or sharp mandibles, they are able to raid insect colonies, create disaster amongst spiders, bees and certain types of insects. In fact, they create such a ruckus in their local environment that some of the creatures that they are hunting are declining in numbers and are slowly failing to their doom. This is not restricted to one part of the world. They have large communication network all over the world such as America and Asia. Argentine ants are even affecting the kings of the world- us Humans!

You see, they have started taking over the local fields and farming areas across the world. Now we will see how this is affecting us. There are certain types of insect species that affect a fly species known as Aphids. Aphids harm crops and destroy these farming areas. Argentine ants hunt the creatures eating the Aphids. This means the Aphid population is going up of the number of insect population is declining. But argentine ants don't stop at this. They started invading human kitchens are dining halls and stealing food from there. And I am not talking about a single grain of salt. I mean they are stealing mass quantities of food like cheese, tomatoes and crumbs of burger. In fact, argentine ants have one of the biggest population in the world. But instances where argentine ants have battled each other have been reported. For example: the lake Hutchins super colony has been fighting against really large super colony for some time now. Furthermore, a group of red exported fire ants were taken to Alabama. They also can make super colonies and have exterminated the argentine ants in that region. Fire ants are much bigger and stronger than argentine ants and when their number comes close to the argentine ants, they will destroy them with ease.

*Argentine ants or any other ant species for that matter, their colonies have a certain uniqueness in their genome. So each ant colony has a different genome.

ARMY ANTS

Army ants usually don't keep burrows like other ants. Instead they around below trees for a while and move on. The army ants sometimes go in millions. Army ants are big and have strong and powerful armour. Their mandibles can snap shut faster than you can blink. In fact, they have so many soldiers that other ants don't even stand a chance. So it is necessary for the other ants to hide. Sometimes, ants have square head to block their entrances so that army ants cannot enter. One army ant colony and another wont battle each other as both the very ferocious army ant colonies will lose the battle. Army ant colonies are so powerful that within minutes of entering another ant's home, they usually plunder and swarm the place, trying to get as close to the larva as possible. Once they do they take too with it at once. This is true for most ants except for the smart and civilized leaf cutter ants.

Leaf Cutter Ants

Leaf cutter ants are vast in numbers and have a complex way of living. Their life style is very similar to the termite. This may sound strange, but their colonies are very similar to ours. Of course there are soldier ants and worker ants. But there is a small group of ants which resemble human servants, at least in social ranking. You see, these leaf cutter ants are very small and do one job no other ant can- remove ticks from the worker's body. Now, let's talk a bit about how they gather food. Well, this is what they do. Every day, from morning to night, workers accompanied by soldiers gather food supplies such as leaves. They then take them to their underground burrows where they pass them on to the little ants. These ants then take the leaf and wrap it around fungus. For ants, fungus is as important as fruits and vegetables are for us. So by eating it in this way, they create a sort of fungus farm.

Finally, we will get to the rank which we didn't mention in the start.

Queens- We all know that there are queen ants. They are very big and fat and never move except for an emergency. The larvae of these giant ant queens are mobile on air. This is how they branch out and find different places to make colonies.

Disclaimer: Some of the things said might scare children under 6!

Slaver Ants

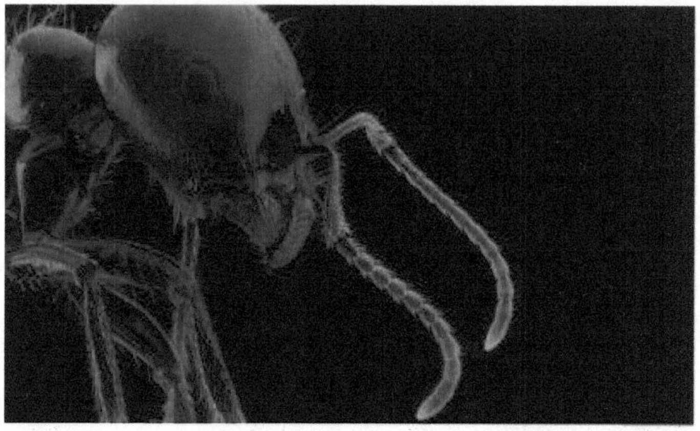

Slaver ants are very strange insects as they cut out most of the perks of being an insect and they go for one perk and dial it up a notch, what is this perk you ask well its *chemical warfare* and this is what got they their name, now I'm switching to situation mode:

There is a colony of army ants in a clearing, these ants are being spied upon by a slaver ant, this slaver ant shall report back to the colony, the slaver ant colony will set for the clearing. Once it has arrived it shall break through the enemy lines, and this where chemical warfare comes in handy: as to get to the objective (eggs) they need to preserve as many members as possible so they send of irritating pheromones to confuse the army ants and they get to the eggs once they get back to their colony they rub their own pheromones on to the larvae, brainwashing them into thinking that they are slaver ants!

And this is of course because pheromones are different in each colony so when the larvae find that the other ants match their pheromone, they think they're in that colony, so slaver much on ants use they're unsuspecting slaves to get food and feed them, slaver ants depend so slaves that they don't know how to eat so they need slaves to feed them. The brainwashing is not The only way the colony can get slaves. They can also get slaves by having the queen kill the other colonies queen and put that queen's pheromone on her so that the colony thinks she is they're.

Jaguar

Jaguars are the masters of stealth! When someone asks you to name the most powerful cats, you would either say lion or tiger or perhaps Cheetah. Well, I'd like to say that the Jaguar is a better hunter than all these 3 cats. Its spotted body allows it to sit comfortably amongst bushes without being spotted. What's more, jaguars are great swimmers. You see, the so called fact that cats hate water only applies to typical everyday cats. This is because the city cat's ancestor the East African wild cat is not used to a large amount of water. But as for the Panthera* family, they are well equipped swimmers. One major difference between a jaguar and a tiger is that the jaguar sacrificed some of its power for aquatic movement. Its powerful arms and legs paddle it through the water much like an otter. Anyway, this ability is useful when catching caimans. A jaguar's body is almost invisible under water.

So, it can quickly come and snap at the caiman's neck or snout. After this, it just needs to send a series of blows at the caiman for it to die. Now, jaguars also can defeat the caiman on land. That is if it's close to the water. There, the jaguar can use its retractable claws to catch hold of the mud, then when in the right position can use it to slash at the caiman's eyes or neck. For those who don't know, it catches the mud for better grip. Now, when I say the word jaguar, you think about a black giant cat. Well, you may have forgotten that there are jaguars in a de-saturated yellow colour and these were the original jaguars. Then, as more plant life started growing in the amazon jungle, they gradually started to grow darker skin because it would help then hide inside the thick shrubbery better.

* The Panthera family is a family separating small city cats from lions and tigers. Small everyday cats are known as Felidae whereas big cats are known as Panthera.

GIANT RIVER OTTER

S ome of you are wondering what is an otter! Otters belong to the mustelids family (A family of creatures that include the honey badger and wolverine). Now, most mustelids have two things that make them a top predator. Ferocity and strength. The honey badger holds the record for being the fiercest mustelid in the world while wolverines are the strongest mustelids in the world. Now you might think that the otter has both, but in reality it has- none! The otter actually survives in a group. I'll just explain to you what I mean in this fun little scenario.

A group of otters comes to drink water in a river. As they start to swim, and drink till their stomachs are full. Suddenly this little group was attacked by an alligator. It opened its mouth showing razor sharp teeth. The otters, although frightened, come up to the alligator. They attack it from all sides biting at the tail, mouth, nose, wherever they can get a good bite. Then the alligator is forced to retreat into the water!

Otters are smart creatures. They can tell between members of their own family and invaders! You see, otters live in groups like a kingdom. When an otter picks a piece of land, it stays to that land till it dies. If an otter wanders off into another piece of land, it is most likely that it is coming to plunder. Most times, it is the offenders that win.

Fun fact: Otters live both in the amazon jungle and in swamps.

BASILISK LIZARD

Lizards can run. They can run on land, they can run through tree tops, they can also jump! They can jump away from predators, above small bodies of water, and more! But have you ever seen a lizard run on water? You immediately might say, "Of course I've not because they can't! Well, you're wrong. There is a special type of lizard called the Basilisk that can quite literally run on water and in this segment, I am going to show you why and more importantly, how. Now, to answer the first question, let's look at the Basilisk's place in the food chain.

So, Basilisks are neither top predators nor at the bottom of the food chain. Basilisks are insectivores, meaning they consume insects and then they get consumed by birds like the bald eagle or the harpy eagle. So, the reason Basilisks do this is that they can escape these predators but this does leave them vulnerable to caimans. But their strategy relies on there being bigger prey to distract the caimans. Now to the best question, 'how'.

Now, there is no one single reason for this question. Many variables come together to allow this mind blowing ability. First one is speed, because if you run very fast, your steps will be barely touching the water so, you won't have time to sink or drown. However, speed itself is not enough. Try running as fast as you can in your swimming pool, you'll sink. We'll tell you why in a moment. The second thing you need are big feet to spread your weight across the water more evenly. Now, think about it like this. Let's say you have a very big mat. Then you put it inside a swimming pool. Will this sink or float? Of course it will float. Then let's say you take the same mat and then fold it and tie it up. It's weight will be the same but all that weight is focused on a smaller area, so it sinks. This is the reason knives are so effectives at piercing things compared to a hammer. If you hit a pillow with a hammer, nothing will happen. But if you take a knife and stab a pillow, then you would have created a hole inside the pillow. This is because the knife has all its force pointed at one small area. So more force is there on that areas. Whereas the hammer has less force because the weight is spread out instead or being concentrated. So, think of the basilisk like the hammer. This is the reason basilisks have wide feet. But even this is not enough. If you stand on 2 tin big plates that are glued to your feet, you'll still sink, which is where the nest step comes in and that is, air bubbles. Let me explain. The basilisks have tiny little mountain like objects on their feet. What I mean is, imagine a small mountain. Then imagine a valley. Now imagine the mountain is curved. Then imagine that there are many mountains like that. Very small mountains that are sitting on the basilisk's feet. So, what do these things do? Well, every time the basilisk goes inside the water, these things close and release air bubbles. (Air bubbles appear when a heavier object pushes air away inside the water. For eg: when you clap your hands inside the water, have you ever seen bubbles coming? I think you have, these are air bubbles. When you jump inside the water, have you seen bubbles coming up? These are also air bubbles. But air also has weight and these air bubbles being produced under the basilisk's feet lift it up slightly. So every time the basilisk's leg goes inside the water, it pushes it up slightly. But even if you add air bubbles to the equation, then you still won't be able to run on water. This brings us to the last but not least point. As basilisk is small and that means it weighs less. So it is running at a certain speed, that speed is ok for its weight. If a human would have to do that, he would have to run at triple the speed of the basilisk. The same thing applies to the others. You need more air bubbles coming up to keep him up on the water. So, since the basilisk is light, it can do this. For humans to do it, they would need to do everything the basilisk is doing, but triple the energy. Only then can we say that a human could run on water.

Note: The basilisk is one example of the ways animals surprise us with their strange tricks and antics. This is another reminder that like humans, all animals have a special power. In other words, don't have too much pride, for your intelligence is only one air bubble in the millions of air bubbles produced under the basilisk lizard's feet.

This is the home of some of the most endangered creatures...

Asia

Bengal Tiger

Tigers in general rule over the environment they inhabit. But as for Bengal Tigers, their numbers are taking a sharp decline due to regular poaching. For this reason, most Bengal tigers are found in wild life reserves, but for the few of them who still manage to survive in the wild, they are a force to be reckoned with. Tigers dominate land and water. Unlike the jaguar, it is simply too heavy to negotiate the tree tops without breaking its skull. But, it has a decent enough jump, which can reach most tree dwelling mammals. Their excellent strength allows them to be quite persistent hunters. While its sense of smell is not as good as say, the Komodo dragon, its good enough in its home server of Asia. The tiger's ancient ancestors such as the sabre tooth, dwell in cold climates. Most tigers, with the exception of the Siberian tiger, like to dwell in tropical climates as this means they don't have to worry about large animals. Most creatures in the arctic or any cold region for that matter, almost always have more fat to store heat. Due to this, animals living in cold climates are usually bulkier. So it would be highly inadvisable for the tiger to waste all its energy on a bulky animal which could possibly trample, stomp or pierce it. Tiger are also the largest feline in the world, with the exception of cross bred animals such as the liger! (mix of the tiger and lion)

Fun fact: All tiger stripes are different.

Asian Elephant

I was talking about the African elephant in the, previous mention. Now we will be talking about the Asian elephant. There are certain differences, between the African and Asian elephant. It's mostly their size. African elephants are a bit larger and have longer tusks. They also have larger ears which, if you remember correctly, are in the shape of the African continent. While Asian elephants are much smaller and weigh less. Now, one of the key parts of any elephant is their intelligence. Most of you may not know that elephants are intelligent. Most importantly, they have feelings i.e. they are sentient. They can feel and think just like humans. For example, their tool use. They sometimes meticulously craft objects to fit their need. Elephants can take a stick to swat a few flies, just like humans. They can use their trunk to grab things and also use them as weapons as their trunk has superior grip and flexibility than any human hand, so they can actually take large branches, huge metallic poles, or just some sticks and swirl them around and hurl or hit its predators. This is another great example of the usefulness of the trunk. The trunk, also acts as a tube with which it can suck water and then put inside its mouth. This is a safer alternative to bending down and sipping as it leaves the weak parts vulnerable to attacks. The elephant can also use its trunk to lift things from the ground. This goes in conjunction with its tool use as it can rip branches from trees or list up rocks to hurl at its opponent. The main reason for the elephant's intelligence could be its trunk as its trunk allows it to maintain balance and still be able to crat objects.

Now let's talk about another interesting feature which is possessed by many animals. This is a nice time to clear up a common misunderstanding. Horns, are when a pierce type weapon is located above the mouth. Tusks are when a piercing type weapon is growing out of an animal's mouth.

Elephants possess tusks. These tusks are used to counter the rhinoceros's horns and vice versa. It's also good for piercing an enemy, preferably a carnivore. Also, this tusk can be used to break termite mounds although the elephant never has the need to do that. All of these things going in conjunction with its big size, grant the elephant control over Asia and Africa. In fact, one of its only weaknesses are to find food to sustain its large size.

Orangutan

The orangutan is the third smartest ape in the world and the only one in Asia. It is red in colour with an orange beard and muscular frame as well as high dexterity and intelligence.

The orange ape is a solitary animal choosing to only meet when mating. its high intelligence allows it to teach its kin to swing on wines, what are the right berries to eat, who to stay away from. Impressive right? But this is not the full extent of its capabilities! Orangutans have been observed to eat medicine that have been made by them {I mean crushed leaves for muscle sore}. Intelligence is not the only thing that makes the orangutan an interesting animal: its strength also allows it to get the spotlight! It has an extra, long and thick bone in its arm. This makes it as strong as five men. A one- year old orangutan is as strong as a human.

DHOLE

A Dhole is a dog-like animal whose features match those of a dog. But this animal is not a dog. It belongs to a group of animals called Cuon. The dholes are an endangered species. They live in India and they dominate the area near the forests. Inside India, in Madhya Pradesh are the last few dholes remaining in the wild. So as you can imagine, they need to keep their heads up for predators. This brings us to the dhole's signature ability- team work and co-operation. The dhole's ability to work as a team give them a recognized place in India as the only animal brave enough to take on a tiger. The dhole's maneuvers and team co-ordination allow it execute perplexing tasks such as helping trapped cubs out of a landslide, natural disaster and dealing with a tiger or leopard. They have many howls that don't sound like howls at all. They are a series of irritating sounds that tell the other dholes that they are in trouble. In short, they are an extremely endangered animal which require human protection to save them

After this we're going to return to the ocean to look at what's deep down at the depths

OCEAN- PART 2

Now we have covered a lot about the animals inside the ocean. But I haven't talked a lot about how people know what's inside the ocean. Like, how do people know that the Mariana trench is there without even looking at it and identifying the width and depth of it. I'm going to answer these questions. Here's a cool fact- If you look at the water in the ocean, then you can see the structure under the water. What I mean is, if there is a piece of raised ground under the water, then the ocean will be raised in that area. Now let's just get back to the animals.

ZONES OF THE OCEAN

For those who don't know, there are 5 zones in the ocean and they are - sunlight zone, twilight zone (these 2 zones are the ones w e have covered in the previous visit to the ocean). After the twilight zone, there is the midnight zone. This is where most large creatures start disappearing and this is also the maximum point that the sperm whale can reach. After this we enter the abyssal zone. Here rest the very weird creatures and it's also the place of glowing lights. Then we have the Hades zone. This zone basically refers to the great trenches of the ocean like the Mariana trench.

Midnight Zone

Dumbo Octopus

The Dumbo Octopus is a strange looking creature in the fact that its head is twice the size of its body. It has all the wonderful traits of a normal octopus, just that its white in colour and its eyes are a faint blue colour.

Cookie Cutter shark

What is a cookie cutter shark you ask? It is basically a small shark witch Razor sharp teeth that bites a cookie shaped bit out of anything it sees.

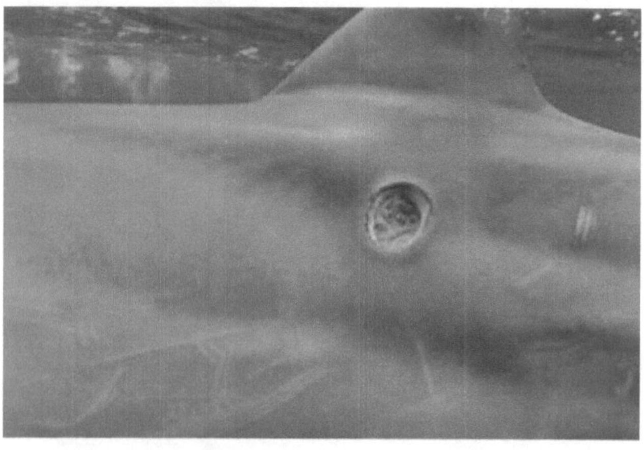

(Bite of a cookie cutter shark)

GIANT SQUID

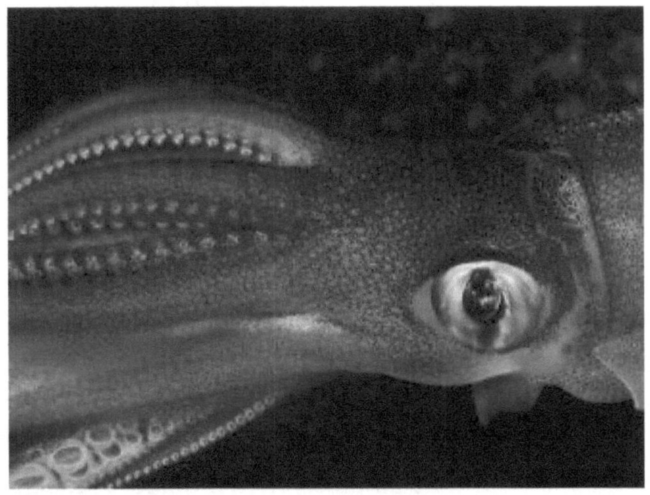

Giant squids have eyes as big as a soccer ball! They also have a beak in the middle of their tentacles. Now is a great time to clear out a common misunderstanding. *All of the squid's tentacles are not tentacles!!!* The two large ones on the side are known as arms and the rest are tentacles. Squids are also very powerful creatures and easily dominate the food chain as their only competition are the sperm whales and orcas. This is mostly because of the fact that the squid's skin is soft and stretchy like rubber, so you cannot pull off limbs from this creature! Biting will also be of little use, as their rubbery texture can withstand huge wear and tear. So the only real way to defeat a giant squid is to get in your mouth. This is also not very easy as while the tentacles are pretty easy to get inside your mouth, the giants arms will be wrapped around your body, stretching itself so that it can get out of your mouth. It also has serrated sharp patterns on its arms and tentacles. Meaning, it also has one of the strongest grips in the world. This is actually a huge contrast to its slimy and stretchy skin.

SPERM WHALE

Sperm whales are the second largest whales in the world and the loudest animals in the world. They create a sound that bounces off the object it touches and gives them a clear idea of water and the animals present. This is called echo location. They eat squid, but they mostly fight with squid to protect the young ones. Many sperm whales can be seen with marks of squid tentacles because squid have razor sharp teeth on their suckers. Humans have never seen a battle like that. Sperm whales often get stuck in ghost nets. Ghost nets are fishing nets that float across the ocean like ghosts after being cut off from the fishing line.

Abyssal Zone

Dragon Fish

Dragon fish are extremely tiny (roughly 1 inch), they're not fast either, so what makes them special? Well dragon fish use bioluminescence to A) attract animals using the glowing fishing rod, and B) give off UV light* to make itself invisible.

*Light that has a high frequency is called UV and light that has a low frequency is called IR light, but what is a frequency? Well a high frequency is where the light rays are close together and move fast, whereas a low frequency is when the light rays move very far from each other and move slow. There is something else called wavelength, so a wavelength measures the width of the wave, now red has a long wavelength but low frequency, and violet has a short wavelength but high frequency, do you get it? UV- Ultra Violet, IR- Infrared. Light that is in the in the in the visible range balances these things with little difference is visible light

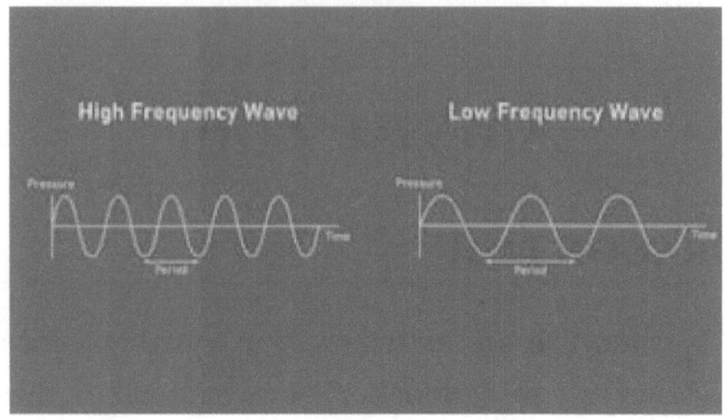

HADES ZONE

YETI CRAB

In the bottom of the hades zone there lives a crab that is hairy and eats germs. Let me explain: so there are millions bacteria on the rock that float across the water, these bacteria have proteins! The crab collects them in its hairs (and filters it) presto! That enables the crab to have energy. This is the only animal known to live in the hades zone.

After visiting all the zone, we will now look at animals that are found all over the world...

TARDIGRADE

Imagine a microscopic creature many times bigger than a virus but smaller than the smallest ant. This living thing is small and you might expect that I am talking about a microbe like bacteria or amoeba. But these creatures are much more fascinating. Nicknamed the water bear, tardigrades are the weakest and the easiest to crush organism on the planet. Literally without knowing, every time you take a step on the ground, you are killing hundreds of tardigrades. Then you might think, why wasn't this creature extinct millions of years ago. Well, if the only fascinating thing about it is its size, then it would have been, but it has an ability that allows it to survive on this earth- which is, extreme survivability! Scientists are not quite sure how tardigrades do it. But, they go into a coma of some sort whenever there is a lack of heat or moisture. This coma state allows them to survive in pressure cookers and microwaves, even a bonfire or the kitchen the stove. This coma also allows them to survive in Antarctica, a freezer and even the immense pressure of the ocean floor (which is absolutely bonkers since it is not even able to withstand a simple touch!) and then, the most amazing thing about tardigrades is the fact that they can live in outer space in their coma state! Scientists are still unable to solve the mystery of the tardigrade but they'll keep searching and when there is an answer, it will help humanity to explore the amazing worlds whether it's under the ocean or the black void engulfing this planet, which we call space!

Note: Right after typing this I stumbled upon a documentary. It said that scientists have revealed some of the secrets of the extreme tardigrades. In hot conditions, the genes of the tardigrade activate special proteins that replace water. This allows it to live in extreme heat in its coma. And for the extreme cold it's probably the same except that the fat or something is being activated. That last point (about extreme cold) was just me making logical assumptions.

Scientists have also discovered other proteins that protect the DNA. This explains how tardigrades are able to casually trot throughout space which is full of radiation that would attack your genes.

EARTHWORM

Earthworms are creatures that have a curious little habit that make observant people, well.. curious! This curious habit is the arrival of an earthworm whenever it rains. At first you might say, the underground will get flooded that's why they come up to the surface. But you'll be surprised to know, earthworms can live under water (as in, ponds) quite well by going into a sort of coma like the tardigrade. But it of course does not have the same extreme coma that the tardigrade has. It's more of a nap. So, it's not that they can't swim. As I was doing this, I asked my mother this question. And she said, 'to get water', which is not far off from the answer. Take a pause here if you want and think for some time. Then read on to see if you are correct.

Have you thought? Well, you're right if your answer was worms need cool places to live or else they'll dry out and get de-hydrated. The reason for this is that there is a sort of earthworm lotion or gel which covers them completely that keeps them cool. But when they are outside for extended durations of time, they would slowly de-hydrate and die. You might say, hold on, it lives underground, so why does it need to worry about the Sun? Well it's because there are predators that are under the earth as well as above the earth. When it rains, the outside air is already cool, so it can venture outside as all the predators have gone. So the rain is the only time the worms can come out freely.

Komodo Dragon

The komodo dragon lives on the island of Komodo. It is extremely powerful and has a deadly venomous bite. The only things that are more impressive than these are its amazing sensory skills. But before I tell you about that, I should tell you how it uses its sensory skills and now would be best time to switch to scenario mode.

A komodo dragon lays in wait next to the river waiting for prey and then, there comes a buffalo. It sips the water, unware that it's in danger. Suddenly, the komodo jumps and lands a venomous bite on the large bovine*. But it runs away and you might think well, the komodo dragon failed, it let its prey escape! Well, that's where you' re wrong. In a week or so, the large horned animal shall perish. Now you might say, if it perishes in a week, how can the komodo dragon find it? It is because it has a very well developed sense of smell, or should I say, taste. Because it sticks it's tongue out and tastes the smell molecules. That means it is sort if 'smell tasting'!

Note: I told you before that the komodo dragon has very little competition. Well, by very little I meant 1 and that is, Humans! Tan tan tannnnn!. They continuously hunt komodo dragon eggs which leaves this species endangered. So remember, take care of nature, which would take care of komodo dragons!

*Cow family

SPIDER

Bird eating spider, aka the Goliath Tarantula inhabits South America. Native to rain forests, this terrifying behemoth completely eliminates competition. There are a few creatures in the area which can match up to the sheer strength and power of this creature and even possibly more strength, like cows. But there are a few special abilities and traits that make the tarantula one of the creepiest beings to ever inhabit planet earth. Now first, before we start talking about the special abilities of the tarantula, we will first break down spiders into three categories. House spiders, venomous spiders and giant spiders. We will look at house spiders first, then work our way to giant spiders. (The tarantula is venomous so don't get confused if you hear that later).

House spiders are very small. They do not have any successful defensive capabilities and their only feasible prey would be small insects like flies. Because of this and their low defensive capability, they generally don't fare well against the largest creatures like birds or small mammals. But, of course not all house spiders are like that.

Some spiders like the golden silk orb weaver spider is known for its special ability which is, its great architecture. It was one of the first animals which unlocked architecture. Its webs are always designed very nicely in a way that they have the support of physics. What I am talking about is that, 1) its web is very sturdy and 2) the web center is especially sticky so that if an insect flies right into the center, the web wouldn't break as, if something hits the web at the center, the force of the impact is spread across the web. Usually this would be a bad thing, as this means all of the parts get damaged. But in the case of the orb weaver spider, it has an especially sticky center which means that the fly can't break the web and fly right through! Also, you might not believe this, but orb weaver spiders have actually parachutes!! These parachutes catch the air and allow the orb weaver spider's offspring to float in the air and avoid the risk of running into dangerous predators and allows them to search for places they can nest in.

Venomous spiders- They are found in America and also Australia. Australia contains one of the most dangerous spiders- the black widow. Its poison can kill a person and can deliver serious damage to any creature that is much bigger. Because of this, they fit quite well into the number of killing machines Australia seems to host.

Giant Spiders- The Goliath Tarantula is no doubt the best spider that you can be, as it has venom that runs through its veins. This venom can deliver a deadly bite to any creature that messes with it. Due to its large size and furry body, plus its large fangs, it's also known to hunt birds. A much feared predator species has now become a spider's prey! It also, uses its fur as a weapon. The Goliath tarantula can sense if there's trouble, then it continuously rubs its back which sends a few urticating hairs towards the direction of the trouble. These urticating hairs are very irritating when latched on to your body.

Coyote

Coyotes are very adaptable. They are quite clever. they steal food from vultures and any other scavenger for that matter. They live anywhere, on the prairie, in the snow, in deserts, tropical Islands and even your back yard. In deserts, they steal food from scavengers. In the cold and icy places near the poles they have thick coats which they used to keep themselves warm. They dig under the snow to find moles. On tropical Islands coyotes wait patiently for sea turtles to lay their eggs. Once the sea turtles leave, the coyote eats the eggs.

The coyote is smart, clever and most of all, a great hunter. Now of the most fascinating and also unnerving point of the coyote is that it's not working alone! There is a small grassland called the prairie which coyotes inhabit. Now in the prairie, there are these creatures called prairie dogs which are actually small squirrels which live in small burrows and caves. The honey badger also lives in the prairie. Its great at hunting things underground while the coyote is great at hunting things above ground. See where I'm going with this? So the coyote forms an alliance with the badger so that prairie dogs which run inside the burrows will be caught by the badger and those who run outside will be caught by the coyote. As far as scientists are concerned, coyotes are the only animals who form an alliance with another predator. Also, they are great at evading traps and stealing. This is mostly because of their soft paws and their stealthy nature. Coyotes use this element while hunting and foraging.

This combined with the usual special abilities of a dog such as superior hearing or smell make the coyote one of the most successful animals of the world. Coyotes also understand traps. They are actually known to avoid or even set traps. Mostly by using created traps to their advantage by stealing the prey that gets caught in the trap set by humans. This level of intelligence is stunning!

Fun fact: Now, I'll take moment here to appreciate how smart the coyotes are. It has unlocked some sort of tool use and because it is teaming up with other animals, it might use their special abilities to its advantage. So soon there's no telling what the coyotes could accomplish!

Speaking of intelligence: we can't not talk about......

Human Being

Human beings dominate the area and are very much the top species currently. But it was not always like that. Let's take a look at how humans became the leaders of the world. It all started in Africa and Asia, where a few apes lived in peace. Although I wouldn't quite say peace as they were literally the lowest creatures on the food chain. They got completely massacred by everything else and their only escape was the arboreal zone (Tree tops). At this point they had neither gotten intelligence or specialized strength of any kind. So as you can see, they were not competition for anyone. It is around this time that humans started walking upright and the reason for this is, they could scan the area much more efficiently. Fast forward to few more years, humans were not as helpless as they were before. They used to eat small pieces of fruit but now, they are eating the left overs of predators like lions by using sharp rocks to break through the bone and get to the marrow. But even now, they wouldn't stand a chance against lions and hyenas. But then, everything changed! There was a giant ICE AGE, but it became hotter in Africa. So, humans needed to survive off fishing which meant they needed to co-operate and share more with each other. Plus, they completely got rid of their hair except for few strands on their heads. This enabled them to dissipate heat more efficiently while sweating. In the meantime, the humans in Asia had migrated to Europe and became known as the Neanderthals. They had longer bodies, stronger muscles and surprisingly a bigger brain than homo sapiens (There were once 6 human species- Homo Sapiens, Homo Neanderthals, Homo Denisova, Homo Luzonesis, Homo Floresiensis and Homo Erectes).

Homo- sapiens then moved to Europe through boats. There they encountered the Neanderthals. The first time sapiens met Neanderthals, they retreated. Scientists are not sure why. But then they came back, smarter than ever using ranged weapons like the spear or *atlatl*. The reason spears are great is that they allow the user to attack the target (by throwing) while still not being in the reach of a counter attack. Neanderthals are large so they can take a few hits so they don't need range weapons but this means they have a greater probability of failure as they can get hurt or even die. Plus, sapiens travel in the hundreds.

Note:

We are the top species but we take too much pride. As in we don't look after our earth and I'm telling you that we're going to die if we don't take of nature. I wrote this book in the hope of showing you the wonders of the natural world and the how everything is connected. In other words: If you cut one strand of the orb weaver's web, everything will come crumbling down...

The end

By Darsh Sathchith

Quiz Time

1. Where do the polyps sleep during day time?

2. What is a tenrec?

3. When do tarantulas shoot out hairs?

4. Why is the octopus considered to be the best at concealing iitself?

5. Is there a way for animals on earth, to survive in space. If so wich one?

6. Which is your favorite chapter?

7. Which is your least favorite chapter?

8. Did you enjoy unlimited nature?- If so, write to us with your thoughts –

Mail id: matha.krish@gmail.com